Poems on Values to Succeed Worldwide in Life: Wonders and Co-operation

Simple and Insightful

O.K. FATAI

Pubished by OK Publishing

Wellington, New Zealand

Copyright © 2019 O.K. Fatai

Email: OK.Publishingnz@gmail.com

Full catalogue information may be obtained from the National Library of New Zealand

All rights reserved.

The moral right of the author has been asserted

ISBN-13: 978-0-4734770-7-3

All rights reserved. No part of this publication may be reproduced, stored in a retrieval system or transmitted in any form by any means electronic, mechanical, photocopying, recording or otherwise, without prior permission from the publisher.

DEDICATION

To all those who like to wonder daily and keep of not only asking questions, but thinking of solutions as well.

Contents

Its beauty	10
It is there	11
When we wonder	12
We sail	13
Understanding love	14
Not confined	15
Disabilities	16
Challenges	17
Rewards	18
Smile	19
Achieving the unimaginable	21
Achieving together	22
There is	23
An orchestra	24
Like a game	25
When we	26
In life	27
There is moving forward	28
We can't stop	29

Network of energy	30
Other books by O.K. Fatai	31
More books by O.K. Fatai	32
About the Author	34

ACKNOWLEDGMENTS

Family, friends and others who keep on wonderings and coming up with solutions that solve issues we encounter daily.

Success Worldwide in Life through Wonderings

Its beauty

The beauty of wonder
lies not in its mystery

but in the ability to envision
the ability to dream

the ability to dare
for without great dreams
we will not be achieving great things.

O.K. FATAI

It is there

While many things lay hidden
and waiting for us to discover

and often what lies hidden
it right there in front of us

and there are many mysteries in life
that were right in front of us

but we have not discovered them
because we don't wonder enough

for there is beauty in the minds that wonder
for often the answers that are right

in front of us are discovered by those
who dare to wonder all the time.

When we wonder

There is a connection between wonders
and the ability to understand
when we wondered

we are on the gate to understand
for the first step to understanding

the mysteries of life and the universe
comes from a mind that asks questions

and seeks answers to those questions
it is the ability of human being

to wonder and seek answers to questions
that has brought us to where we are now.

We sail

We sail in the sea of life
sometimes we encounter storms

and the challenges of life
and while it is inevitable that

there are storms in life
we shouldn't let them

stop us from dreaming
and envisioning the great goals

we are sailing towards
for they are the goals that

will ultimately define our destiny
for we must never stop

our eagerness to wonder
even through the many storms
we encounter in life.

Understanding love

When we wonder
we will come to understand

some of the many unanswered
questions that we seek to know

and often when we wonder
we begin to understand

the greatness of love
the benefits of forgiveness

the goodness of mercy
and the abundance of grace

and the more we wonder
the greater our understanding

of why we are really here.

O.K. FATAI

Not confined

We are sometimes confined
to the wonders of the adults
and people we know

we are sometimes confined
to the wonders of the elite in society
we are sometimes confined

to the wonders of the educated few
we are sometimes confined
to the wonders of the CEOs

we are sometimes confined
to the wonders of the managers
and while these are important

we should also rate as equally
important in life
the wonders of the homeless

the wonders of the little children
the wonders of the unemployed
for sometimes the great advancement

that we have today
were the results of wonders
by people considered unimportant by society.

Disabilities

We are sometimes struck by some kind
of disabilities as we journey in life

some of these disabilities are temporal
and others are permanent

and while disabilities make us struggle in life
we should never underestimate the power

of wonders by those who are limited in some way
for some of the greatest in this world

were people who had disabilities
and the world had changed for the better

because of the wonders of people with disabilities
and yes there are so many of them out there

continuing to wonder great dreams and visions
and how to make this world a better world.

O.K. FATAI

Challenges

Some of the wonders that we have
were the results of thinking by smart people

and while these are great
it is equally great to see the amazing wonders

of people who go through challenges in life
for sometimes the darkest times in life

can be the catalyst needed for the greatest wonders
for challenges are like mountains we climb

even though it is hard to go up mountains of challenges
it is equally a blessing and helpful to climb

and not to mention the blessings of reaching the top
and see the greatness of the mountain

for sometimes it is in the peak of the mountains in life
that we make the greatest discovery
and the greatest wonders of our lives.

Rewards

There are rewards we have for the wonders we make
there are rewards we have for our thinking and dreams

and while there are so many rewards for great wonders
it is sometimes the little thank you that make the greatest impact

the words of thanks from love ones
the words of gratitude from our children and colleagues

the words of love from our friends and partners
for sometimes greatest the rewards of our wonders

come from those closest to us
not because they have wealth and a lot of money

but because their thank you and their praises
are thank you and praises that come from their souls.

O.K. FATAI

Smile

Smile not because you are wealthy with money
but because you are wealthy with your thoughts

smile not because you are promoted to a CEO position
but because you have made some wonders today

smile not because you have degrees from a well-known university
but because you have some dreams for yourself

smile not because you live in a palace like a king
but because you have some wonders for your family

smile not because you have won the a money draw
but because you have some wonders for the world

sometimes it is the wonders of the ordinary people
in our societies that really make the difference in this world.

POEMS ON VALUES TO SUCCEED WORLDWIDE

Succeed Worldwide in Life through Co-operation

O.K. FATAI

Achieving the unimaginable

We had achieved great accomplishments
just because we worked as a team

and we cannot achieve great results
unless we cooperate and work together

for cooperation shows that we bring
our strength and abilities together

and it is only in cooperation we will
achieve the unimaginable.

Achieving together

Cooperation is about achieving together
it is about reaching our goals as a team

it is about realizing that all is better than one
it is about committing oneself to one another

it is about coming together and working for one another
it is about going hand in hand together

it's about us all rather than one alone.

There is

With cooperation there is immense hope
rather than a wishful hope

with cooperation there is overcoming immense obstacles
rather than overcoming a small challenge

with cooperation there is happiness for all
rather than smiles for an individual

with cooperation there is a winning formula enjoyed by all
rather than just an individual taste of winning.

An orchestra

Cooperation is an orchestra
that makes playing so much more harmony

cooperation is an orchestra
that together, make tunes of beauty and wonders

cooperation is an orchestra
that allows a soloist to excel, but still in context of togetherness

cooperation is an orchestra
that blesses so many because it was done by so many.

O.K. FATAI

Like a game

Like a game cooperation is about winning together
like a game cooperation is about working together

like a game, individuals excel, but still in togetherness
like a game, we face challenges together

like a game, we overcome obstacles together
like a game, we can do so much more

for a game is won by a team working together
and may be one may shine brightly

and a gold medal can be one by one
but there is a team of people

working together behind the scene.

When we

When we cooperate, we don't deny that we may have differences
when we cooperate, we don't deny that we may have contrasting views

when we cooperate, we don't deny that we may have dissimilar opinions
when we cooperate, we don't deny that we may have different insights

but what we do value though is that cooperation achieves a greater aim
cooperation brings a greater value to all of us

cooperation accomplishes more for all of us in life.

In life

In life there are diversities and varieties
in life there are wide ranges and mixtures

in life there are multiplicities and differences
but those are the blessings we have in this life

it is like looking at nature and enjoying the huge
variety of living trees that make nature filled with aliveness

but even though nature has a huge variety of trees
with all its different diversities and collections

they all work together like a team to produce the incredible magic
that enables human life to prosper and filled with life.

There is moving forward

When we cooperate a family can move forward with great pace
when we cooperate a business can strive forward with great speed

when we cooperate a community can go forward with great steps
when we cooperate a country can travel forward with great strides

when we cooperate the world will achieve what had never been achieved before.

O.K. FATAI

We can't stop

We can't stop the contest we have in life
but even with the contest in life, one against another

we can still move forward in cooperation
like a company with staff contesting for different positions

but at the same time working together to achieve profits for the company
the world had grown economically to what we have today

because the world allows companies and countries to contest and be different
but together there is economic progress and it is in togetherness also

that we can lift up countries and citizens that are not as well off as others.

Network of energy

Like a network of computers, energy is transmitted from one to another
cooperation is like that, working differently, but transmitting enthusiasm

from one person to another
like a network of computers, there is interconnection and inter-networking

and just like a network of computers, cooperation is alive and well when
we interconnect and network with one another, contributing what we produce

to the goodness of all.

Other books by O.K. Fatai

1. Poems on Values to Succeed Worldwide in Life: Being Responsible
2. Poems on Values to Succeed Worldwide in Life: Courage
3. Poems on Values to Succeed Worldwide in Life: Good Families
4. Poems on Values to Succeed Worldwide in Life: Forgiveness
5. Poems on Values to Succeed Worldwide in Life: Good Friends
6. Poems on Values to Succeed Worldwide in Life: Grace
7. Poems on Values to Succeed Worldwide in Life: Hope
8. Poems on Values to Succeed Worldwide in Life: Humility
9. Poems on Values to Succeed Worldwide in Life: Joy
10. Poems on Values to Succeed Worldwide in Life: Justice
11. Poems on Values to Succeed Worldwide in Life: Life
12. Poems on Values to Succeed Worldwide in Life: Love
13. Poems on Values to Succeed Worldwide in Life: Mercy
14. Poems on Values to Succeed Worldwide in Life: Peace
15. Poems on Values to Succeed Worldwide in Life: Perseverance
16. Poems on Values to Succeed Worldwide in Life: Faith
17. Poems on Values to Succeed Worldwide in Life: Harmony

with Nature

18. Poems on Values to Succeed Worldwide in Life: Education

More books by O.K. Fatai

1. Poems on Values to Succeed Worldwide in Life: Understanding and Wisdom

2. Poems on Values to Succeed Worldwide in Life: Work and Optimism

3. Poems on Values to Succeed Worldwide in Life: Adversity and Confidence

4. Poems on Values to Succeed Worldwide in Life: Listening and Diversity and Unity

5. Poems on Values to Succeed Worldwide in Life: Sharing and Honesty

6. Poems on Values to Succeed Worldwide in Life: Simplicity and Harmony

7. Poems on Values to Succeed Worldwide in Life: Unity in Diversity and Connections

8. Poems on Values to Succeed Worldwide in Life: Contentment and Acceptance

9. Poems on Values to Succeed Worldwide in Life: Excellence and Compassion

10. Poems on Values to Succeed Worldwide in Life: Generosity and Being Passionate

11. Poems on Values to Succeed Worldwide in Life: Gentle-

ness and Trustworthy

12. Poems on Values to Succeed Worldwide in Life: Patience and Being Tactful

13. Poems on Values to Succeed Worldwide in Life: Purity and Integrity

14. Poems on Values to Succeed Worldwide in Life: Being Modest and Persistence

15. Poems on Values to Succeed Worldwide in Life: Respect and Loyalty

16. Poems on Values to Succeed Worldwide in Life: Self-Discipline and Orderliness

17. Poems on Values to Succeed Worldwide in Life: Service and Going the Extra Mile

18. Poems on Values to Succeed Worldwide in Life: Sincerity and Honour

19. Poems on Values to Succeed Worldwide in Life: Nature and Reliability

20. Poems on Values to Succeed Worldwide in Life: Helpfulness and Consideration

21. Poems on Values to Succeed Worldwide in Life: Preparedness and Visionary

22. Poems on Values to Succeed Worldwide in Life: Reverence and Thankfulness

23. Poems on Values to Succeed Worldwide in Life: Wonders and Cooperation

About the Author

O.K. Fatai is a poet and author from Wellington, New Zealand. He likes to spend time writing poems, especially ones that explore the different aspects of values and virtues that are widely accepted in different cultures today.

O.K. Fatai also likes to write songs and some of his forthcoming books are song lyrics that also look at different values and virtues and some of their appeal to us today. In his spare time, he writes short stories and novels. He is looking forward to sharing these stories with readers around the world, and he has already published some short stories and has more than ten forthcoming publications in children's literature. O.K. Fatai is also writing novels for young adults and adults. He is also a playwright and has written and/or directed more than eight short plays.

He likes painting abstract art and enjoys the different interpretations of abstract paintings, especially when they reflect values and virtues. He is also a photographer who likes to take photographs of nature and the environment, which has a special place in his heart. He is keen on filming and editing videos as well, plays musical instruments and is part of a local band.

O.K. Fatai is a volunteer at the United Nations and regional prisons in Wellington and, for many years, had volunteered to more than ten other organizations. He works in the health sector and is also a consultant for three different online companies, and the President and CEO of more than three businesses. He is also available as an external consultant to the United Nations, the European Bank for Reconstruction and Development, and the Asian Development Bank.

O.K. FATAI

POEMS ON VALUES TO SUCCEED WORLDWIDE

O.K. FATAI

POEMS ON VALUES TO SUCCEED WORLDWIDE

www.ingramcontent.com/pod-product-compliance
Lightning Source LLC
Chambersburg PA
CBHW021413290426
44108CB00010B/518